Let's Dance

Jazz Dancing

By Mark Thomas

Welcome Books

Children's Press
A Division of Grolier Publishing
New York / London / Hong Kong / Sydney
Danbury, Connecticut

Photo Credits: Cover and all photos by Maura Boruchow
Contributing Editor: Jeri Cipriano
Book Design: Michael DeLisio

Visit Children's Press on the Internet at:
http://publishing.grolier.com

Library of Congress Cataloging-in-Publication Data

Thomas, Mark, 1963-
   Jazz dancing / by Mark Thomas.
      p. cm. — (Let's dance)
   ISBN 0-516-23144-8 (lib. bdg.) — ISBN 0-516-23069-7 (pbk.)
   1. Jazz dance—Juvenile literature. [1. Jazz dance.] I. Title.

GV1784 .T56 2000
793.3—dc21

00-043186

Contents

My name is John.

I like **jazz dancing**.

I use my whole body when I dance jazz.

5

I learn how to jazz dance at class.

Other kids like jazz dancing, too.

We dance to fast music.

7

We stand behind the teacher in class.

We watch as she dances.

We follow her **dance steps**.

9

We wear soft shoes.

We wear **leotards**, too.

Jazz dancing uses all parts of the body.

We use our legs.

We use our arms.

We use our heads.

13

Today we are learning the **pike jump**.

We jump and throw out our legs.

We touch our toes.

15

We learned our dance.

Now we will put on a **show**.

We get to dance on a **stage**.

We wear **costumes**.

The music plays and
we dance.

Jazz dancing is fun under
the bright lights.

19

We **bow** when we are finished.

Everybody claps.

Our weeks of **practice** have made us look great!

New Words

bow (**bow**) bending at the waist

costumes (**kos**-toomz) clothes worn for a show

dance steps (**dans steps**) ways to move your feet and body while dancing

jazz dancing (**jaz dans**-ing) dancing that uses the whole body

leotards (**lee**-uh-tahrdz) dance clothes that stretch for easy movement

pike jump (**pyk jump**) a jazz dance move

practice (**prak**-tis) to do over and over

show (**shoh**) when people dance or act before a crowd

stage (**stayj**) a place where shows are put on

To Find Out More

Books
Christy Lane's All That Jazz and More
by Christy Lane
Kendall/Hunt Publishing

Dancing in Your Head: Jazz, Blues, Rock and Beyond
by Gene Santoro
Oxford University Press

Web Site
WorldBook.com—Jazz
http://www.worldbook.com/fun/aamusic/html/listen.htm
You can listen to jazz music and learn more about
different types of jazz.

Index

About the Author
Mark Thomas is a writer and educator who lives in Florida.

Reading Consultants
Kris Flynn, Coordinator, Small School District Literacy, The San Diego County Office of Education

Shelly Forys, Certified Reading Recovery Specialist, W.J. Zahnow Elementary School, Waterloo, IL

Peggy McNamara, Professor, Bank Street College of Education, Reading and Literacy Program